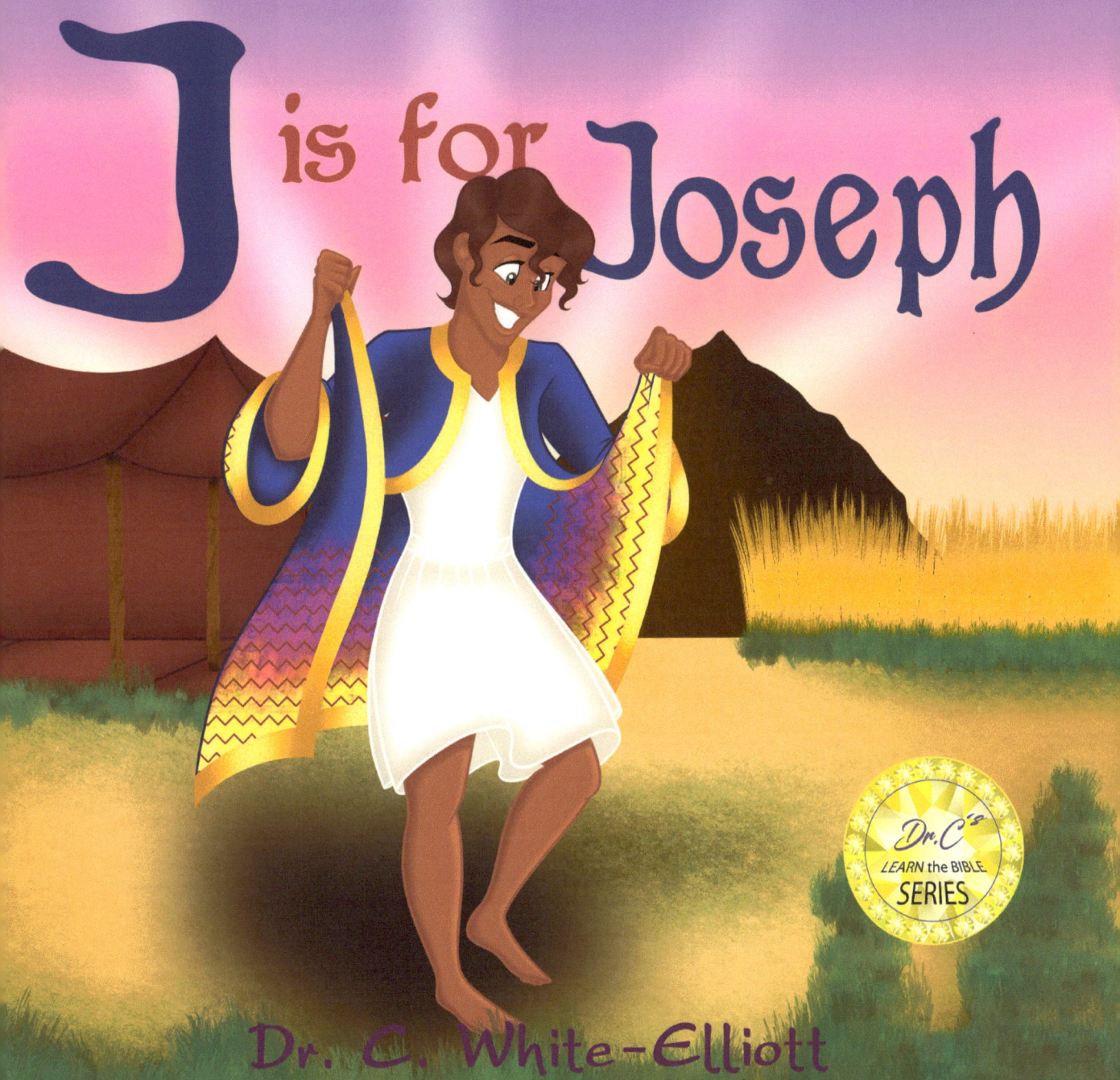

www.clfpublishing.org
909.315.3161

Copyright © 2020 by Cassundra White-Elliott.

All rights reserved. No portion of this book may be reproduced, stored in a retrieval system, or transmitted by any form or any means electronically, photocopied, recorded, or any other except for brief quotations in printed reviews, without the prior permission of the publisher.

Cover design by Senir Design: info@senirdesign.com

Illustrations by Ariel.

ISBN # 978-1-945102-61-5

Printed in the United States of America.

For

London McFarquhar

Joseph was the eleventh son of Jacob, who was the son of Isaac, who was the son of the father of many nations, Abraham.

Jacob & Joseph

Joseph was well loved by his father Jacob. Jacob loved Joseph so much that he gave Joseph a special gift. It was a coat of many colors, and Joseph thought it was very special.

One night, Joseph had a dream about himself and his brothers. In the dream, they were in the field binding sheaves of grain. Then, Joseph's sheaf rose and stood straight up. His brothers' sheaves gathered around his and bowed down, showing honor.

When Joseph's brothers heard the dream, they became very upset. They did not like the idea of bowing down to their younger brother and showing him honor. First, their father had given him the coat of many colors and now the dream! It was too much for them. They plotted to get rid of him.

First, they threw him down a well, hoping to never see him again. When they threw him down the well, they ripped his coat off him. Joseph was just a teenager at that time. He did not understand why his brothers would treat him that way. He was very sad.

Then, Joseph's brothers came up with another idea. They decided to sell him into slavery. So, they grabbed him out of the well and sold him to a group of men who gave him to Potiphar. Joseph became the house servant of Potiphar.

Not much later, Joseph was thrown in prison because his master's wife accused him of harming her. Once again, Joseph did not understand everything that was happening to him, but God was keeping him safe.

Later, when Joseph was an adult, he was taken to Pharaoh to interpret a dream Pharaoh had the night before. After Joseph told Pharaoh what his dream meant, Pharaoh was so impressed, he made Joseph second in command of all of Egypt. See, God was watching over Joseph the entire time!

Many years later, the people in Canaan ran out of food. That was where Joseph's father and brothers lived. So, they had to go to Egypt where Joseph lived to buy food, so they would not go hungry. When they arrived, Joseph was the one they talked to about getting food to eat, but they did not recognize him. And, he didn't tell them who he was.

After Joseph's brothers took food back to Canaan, they went to Egypt again and took the youngest brother Benjamin with them. During that visit, Joseph told his brothers who he was, and they reunited. He was very happy to see his youngest brother, Benjamin.

Later, Joseph's entire family left Canaan and moved to Egypt. Joseph saw his father for the first time in about thirteen years. They hugged, and the entire family was happy that they are all together again.

www.ingramcontent.com/pod-product-compliance
Lightning Source LLC
Chambersburg PA
CBHW041933160426
42813CB00103B/2916